Deborah,
    Change the world
with words — touch
them, breathe them,
Live the beauty of
them!

Day

Black Silk

With a Foreword by Gail Moore, Ed.D.

Shay Cook

iUniverse, Inc.
Bloomington

Black Silk

iUniverse books may be ordered through booksellers or by contacting:

iUniverse
1663 Liberty Drive
Bloomington, IN 47403
www.iuniverse.com
1-800-Authors (1-800-288-4677)

ISBN: 978-1-4759-4059-6 (sc)
ISBN: 978-1-4759-4061-9 (hc)
ISBN: 978-1-4759-4060-2 (e)

Library of Congress Control Number: 2012913532

Printed in the United States of America

iUniverse rev. date: 8/29/2012

Poetry is like black silk—

sumptuous, sensual, soothing, and sinister.

In Memoriam

To the Matriarchs; the Grande Dames:

Ms. Mary Alice Cook, my mother

and

Mrs. Emma Horton, my grandmother

Strong, spirited, ardent, women.

In the strength of your branches I grow, bend, stretch, and drip

with the sweet, syrupy sap of life!

Contents

Foreword

A woman of poetic sensibility, Shay Cook's *Black Silk* defies the opinion that poetry is hard to grasp with little or no relevancy. Poetry is undeniably a private form of articulation and the the poet's need for expression is at the forefront. However, its radiant effects on readers have no limits. Authors' denotations often escape readers, but a willingness to make meaning of poetry can lift readers to heights unknown—spiritually and emotionally. Unfortunately, both young and older adult readers sometimes feel their comprehension is inadequate for private interpretations, robbing them of entry to worthwhile poems.

Throughout my teaching career, a major portion of my students complained that poetry is too abstract for relativity. Students inevitably challenged me at every poetry unit. Arguably, *Black Silk's* collection of poems will lift the veil and convert readers who are averse to poetry. I recognized myself, someone I know, or someone I read about on every page. The writings are easy to dissect and to identify subtleties. Ms. Cook definitely rose to the challenge of mixing words with the right rhythms, metaphors, allegories, imageries and personifications to relate to her audience. As Ms. Cook rises to literary esteem, it is my desire that educators and librarians alike include her works in their must-read collections.

I've long known poetry was Ms. Cook's "golden goose"; she just needed the right forum. Over the years, as I listened to her recite and perform so eloquently her original writings, she never ceased to leave me in awe. *Black Silk* left me breathless! Ms. Cook's creative and eloquent use of words and phrases reminded me of well-known writers like Maya Angelou and Toni Morrison. I hope *Black Silk* is the first of many poetry books.

….Shay, we blended so well as part of the college prayer group on Florida A and M University's campus decades ago. What bonding! I dreamed of the afterglow — so many talented "sorors"… I've had the good fortune of watching you blossom into a poised and graceful woman of God. It is an honor to know and love you.

You are a gift to the world, and to me. - ***Gail Moore, Ed.D.***

Preface

The last time I wore black silk I thought about poetry. I adore silk. I love the smooth, luscious feel of it against my skin. Whether I am donning a blouse or succulent dress, the feeling is the same! Poetry is equally as plush. It is like black silk—sumptuous, sensual, soothing, and sinister. Hence, the title of this book! I was not looking for a cute caption to give to my editing and design team. I sincerely feel this way about poetry and keep these adjectives in my mind's eye when writing.

Black Silk has been simmering in the pot for quite some time while the flavors, smells, and sauces culminated into one delectable dish! It took a little time to brew. Not because I was procrastinating, but because there were experiences still to be lived and captured on these pages!

Black Silk, an anthology of my past and current pieces of poetry and prose, shares life experiences in print—mine and others. In writing *Black Silk* I hope to ignite a renewed allure for poetry, initiating fresh dialogue about this art form.

I truly love literature! I adore words—reading and writing them. There is nothing more exciting to me than coiling on the couch with orange spice tea, Chopin playing in the background, and quill in hand scribbling posh, luscious, mouthwatering words to garnish the universe. How fulfilling!

Through the years, while honing my writing craft, I learned early to keep my heart open to allow the Spirit of creativity to reign supreme—to let the words flow where they will without justifying themselves. In doing so the most sumptuous, sensual, soothing, and sinister pieces of poetry have emanated straight from my soul into my fingers. Turn the pages and savor the opulence of silk against your skin.

Acknowledgements

First, I would be negligent not to acknowledge Jesus Christ, the Lord of my life, who bestowed upon me this beautiful gift of writing. As a Woman of Letters, I count it a joy and privilege that the Lord has entrusted me with his ornate, powerful, meaningful words that deliver souls, soothe hearts, mend disagreements and evoke love.

To my dear friend Dr. Henry L. Porter, Founder of the Westcoast Center for Human Development, what a breath-taking, awe-inspiring journey you and I have traveled these many years! My adoration for words, sentences and punctuation marks begin with you! From the first time you allowed my adolescent feet to stand on the world stage of the Westcoast Center for Human Development to this present moment, you saw inside of me the brilliant, translucent hues that form this luminous kaleidoscope called Shay! Your visionary eyes peeled back my onion layers and pulled from them these opulent, paper leaves. You preached, prayed, and propelled me to this hour! In the publishing of this book, I say thank you. I treasure every word we speak —from our lips and our hearts. When across the crowded room our eyes meet, in them we say everything and know! Lovely, I am your poem!

Thanks to my beautiful sisters, Mae, Nacia, and Sylvia, and my brothers Arthur and Jonathan who's strong, vivacious blood flow rich through my veins. I find comfort in your love and support. You are the warm afghan I wrap myself in.

To the lovely people of Westcoast – men, women and children, whom my heart pants after as the waterfall, I noticed when you hung on every word, applauded, gave standing ovations, were agents of encouragement, and escorted me to the poet's podium. You are most gracious! I cherish and love you.

To my dearest friends of thirty years —Janice Swain, Cynthia Kindred and JS, I share this book with you—you believe in my dreams and awaken them. Yvette German, Andrew Nogueira, Yolanda Cistaro, and Janice Brown, your artistic insight evoked invaluable conversation.

Finally, to my editors and design team at iUniverse, thanks for walking me through every literary step. Kathi Wittkamper you are a consummate professional and genius!

...Sumptuous

Continuously you cloak yourself and sneak inside my poems. I pretend not to notice thoughts of you incessantly.

The Pianist

The notes were playful and plentiful,

Spinning and spiraling on the crisp, clear waves of air,

And they were alluring.

They hovered and danced and bowed,

Then flipped themselves over and upward.

Leaning forward I caught the scent of the love songs as they flew by,

And was filled with joy and delight as the notes grew wings.

Like birds of the air they carried the matter of love straight into my heart

Leaving me faint and weak.

While I stood helpless the pianist juggled each note with his fingers,

Tossed them into the night air with abandon,

Then flung them at me with full force.

I staggered drunk and intoxicated in the aroma of the love songs

While the pianist looked on satisfied.

That pianist was ruthless.

I shall return to him again!

Beautiful

I am the height of the pine tree.

I am crab apple blossoms pirouetting their leaves,

Frosty wind howling through naked willow trees—beautiful.

I am hyacinth moist with June's new rain,

Sleeping Blue Mountains stretching their veins,

Moonlight floating across milky white fields,

I am women in high heels—beautiful.

Beautiful as the aroma of potent perfume,

As the certainty of my steps as I enter the room is beautiful.

Like the stallion in his majesty and hoofs,

As soft as summer rain hitting against tin roofs is beautiful.

Beautiful as winter silhouetted against time,

Beautiful as life sublime,

As a new born cooing,

As romance and wooing,

As sweet and smooth as butter soft kisses,

And hopeful wishes are beautiful.

I am white diamonds, black pearls,

Daddy's baby, mama's girl,

I am the fresh sap on a wet dew morning,

The fiery sunset at evening tide,

I am the arms you run into,

And the peace you find there when they are open wide to you.

I am the place you lodge and the warmth you wrap yourself in,

I am the listening ear and the calm of a gentle friend.

I am full enough to hold your dreams and pain,

And empty enough to fill you up again.

I am enough in all you see,

I am all you need and all I need to be—beautiful.

He's A Man

Look at him gently lying there,
Caramel skin, silky smooth hair,
My heart is in his hands for safe keeping,
Prayer is in his soul while he's sleeping,
He's a man!

He's a hard-working, loving, caring,
Soft-spoken, never swearing,
Kind-hearted, giving, sharing,
Good-looking, blue jean-wearing man.

He's a root beer drinking, chocolate eating,
One woman, never cheating man.
The only cheating that he does,
Is from Sunday church and that's because,
He's plowing the fields, shucking the corn,
Feeding the baby calves that are born.
He's a man!

He's a hard-working, loving, caring,

Soft-spoken, never swearing,

Kind-hearted, giving, sharing,

Good-looking, blue-jean wearing man!

David

Yesterday, a year ago, today, I forget, I bumped into David.

There I was standing on the corner of Tenth and Elm,

My thoughts on a million things to do and light years away from David

When he surfaced on the sidewalk,

Breath swirling hot circles against my shoulders.

He was still beautiful—olive skin, gray flecks of hair, statuesque,

Hovering over me like the skyscrapers surrounding the downtown hub.

He touched me on my elbow with the crispness of snow,

The residue from his fingers dripping with poetry,

Memorable, familiar, recognizable, proverbial.

Then as quickly as he surfaced he disappeared into the crowd,

Leaving me alone with once upon a time and my fingers in my face,

Tracing my lips, wiping my tears, and remembering yesterday,

A year ago, today, I forget.

A Small Still Place

There is a small, still place inside of me,

That is mine and mine alone,

For the safe keeping of my dreams,

For the centering of my soul.

For the rebel, defiant woman mounted on the wild, untamed horse,

Riding the stallion fast for all he is worth.

Airborne atop his strong frame of muscles and power,

I hold the stallion firm as I dare against the wind.

Dust in my face,

Courage in my eyes,

Grit on my teeth,

My legs against his strides,

Unruly blood gushing through my veins,

While he kicks and bucks and jolts and gallops and all that remains,

Is the power of my resistance.

I hold him fast,

I hold him tight,

I hold him strong with all my might,

Until he is broken,

Until he is free,

Until I bring us both to our wildest.

Blow Torch

In the gray misty gloom where withered summer roses,

Clutch a thousand wintry chills,

And frost bitten moments come to paralyze your will,

Breathe.

Breathe visible birds of fate and song,

Breathe yourself into the flute, the piccolo, the violin, that you belong,

Until your fingers know their place,

Like the dancer's feet, weave body through space,

Until your hands know the feel of skin,

As the grace of the poet's pen,

On leaves of silver and brass and string.

Blow until fluid music you bring,

As soft as love and joy and pain,

Then do it all over again.

Open your mouth and breathe.

Like glass blowing in a velvet blur of gold,

Hold on to the visions which gust inside you,

Hold on to the music which glides you,

As a skater's blades on infinite ice.

Blow once, then twice, then thrice,

Until sounds break through your fears and imaginations,

Until your words are more than loud vibrations,

Until you turn your dream into living, liquid form.

Open your mouth and breathe.

Growing Old

When I grew old God was there,

Like a foreign country I had not visited,

Filled with cobblestone streets meandering through lush green valleys

that guided me to quaint little vegetable markets in the heart of town.

There I took in the smells of spices and curry,

Sniffed the newness of the unfamiliar,

Taste-tested foods I had never eaten,

Then filled my basket with succulent delights

To concoct the most scrumptious stew.

Inferno

Does the fire of your dream awaken you?

Does it burn like a torch in the night?

Like flames does it set your soul ablaze?

Like fire does your dream ignite?

Does the dream you once had still follow you?

Does it whisper to your spirit and soul?

Does it lay down with you at midnight?

At daybreak does your dream unfold?

Does the fire of your dream still beckon you?

Does it call to you from black smoke?

Does it linger deep down in your spirit?

Do you still see your dream as hope?

If the fire of your dream still troubles you,

If it hits at you like a fist,

If it beats against your being,

If your dream never gives you rest,

If the fire of your dream still summons you,

If the dream you have never die,

The best thing you can do for your dream,

Is to give it wings to fly!

Cooking Classes

I cut my culinary teeth on the skirt tail of Mama's white cotton aprons,

Drenched in fried fish and day old Crisco oil.

Speckled with corn meal and garlic,

My hands were covered in self-rising flour,

Just pasty enough to coat the fritters.

Burners pre-heated on the cast iron stove,

I learned much about life and love,

Passion spilling over out of every pot,

With wisdom spattered on teachable moments,

Of generous helpings served to a child.

Timeless

Standing close I feel the wind against this frigid sky,

I kick off my shoes, curl on the couch, with me, myself and I.

With lemon tea, a well-read book, I grab my warm afghan,

And nestle beneath the crocheted yarn and think about this man who is timeless.

Timeless as the autumn leaves which dance upon the foliage.

Like summer rain which grows the grain and tulips in the spillage.

Like music, like the painter's brush which strokes his work of art,

As Beethoven and Chopin who plays upon the heart, this man is timeless.

Like violins which pluck their notes and strum in splendid measure,

As melodies and symphonies and words which give me pleasure,

Like a little piece of chocolate, like well fermented wine,

And as the Stradivarius he gets better in his time,

Like Versace and Gucci and Vera Wang,

As Davinci and Latte' and class in simple things, he is timeless.

Timeless like the mustard seed which metamorphose in bloom,

As moonlit nights and candlelight illuminates a room,

Timeless as the Yellowstone and as the Cedar tree,

As New Year's Eve, Auld Lang Syne, and down on bended knee are timeless.

Timeless as the hues in autumn—browns, reds, and yellows,

As daffodils and little feet which scuttle through the meadows.

As days and weeks and months and years and insurmountable hours,

As dogwood trees and maple leaves and scents in orchid flowers,

He is timeless.

Like Versace and Gucci and Vera Wang,

As Davinci and Latté and class in simple things.

He is timeless like the warmth I feel when wrapped in my afghan,

Which comforts me and totals up the measure of this man who is timeless.

Yellow Majesty

A moonlit night.

A sunflower.

A yellow tulip.

Sunrise in its new hour.

Yellow as fire,

As passion's desire,

As sweet lemonade on a summer's eve.

Like an autumn morning, crisp and brisk,

Filled with orange and yellow leaves.

Yellow as the colors in the rainbow,

As gold fish gurgling in a lake,

Like lemon drops and gummy bears,

And banana crème pie for goodness sake!

Like honey bees dancing on golden daffodils,

In a springtime meadow full of children,

Wearing smiles of yellow happiness,

As bright as laughter and lemon fresh air,

As majestic as God and prayer.

Miss Emma's Cooking

Collard greens, corn bread, macaroni cheese,

I wonder why my hips keep looking like these.

There's nothing in the world like a country old woman,

In the kitchen just looking and cooking and plundering.

Pat a cake and bake a cake and put it in a pan,

Roll those fluffy biscuits and pat them in your hand.

Gingerbread, crackling bread, any kind of bread,

Miss Emma gets to cooking whatsoever's in her head.

I know that I can stand to lose a pound or two or three,

But Miss Emma's cooking keeps sabotaging me.

Pound cake, chocolate cake, red velvet cake,

She'll fry it up or stir it up or use her shake and bake.

I know that I can stand to lose a pound or four or ten,

But Miss Emma's cooking makes me come back again.

Lemon crème pound cake, sweet potato pie,

The way that woman cooks, my oh my!

I know that I can stand to lose a pound or twelve or twenty,

But Miss Emma piles my plate with plenty,

Peach cobbler, rice pudding, angel's food cake,

Sweet corn, lima beans, and country fried steak,

I know that I can stand to lose thirty five or forty,

But Miss Emma's cooking, my lordy, my lordy!

Meat loaf, pot roast, and southern fried chicken,

She'll make you smack your lips and your fingers you'll be licking.

I know that I can stand to lose forty-five or fifty,

But Miss Emma's cooking just taste so nifty.

Self-rising flour, corn meal, and cooking oil,

She'll fry it up or bake it up or bring it to a boil.

You know Miss Emma's cooking, it just ought to be a crime,

How that woman bakes from scratch and she can make a key-lime.

There's nothing like a country old woman in the kitchen,

Looking and cooking and carousing and fetching.

I know that at some point at myself I should be looking,

But why do that when I can blame Miss Emma's cooking?

Poetry

I am not merely defined by veins

And blood

And cells

And corpuscles

And tendon,

But am spawned by lines of love,

And joy

And sadness

And laughter

And hurt

And pain

And happiness

That metamorphose into poetry.

Victrola and 78's

I found the record albums and the old victrola

When I was cleaning out my grandfather's life.

They were stored away in vegetable crates,

Protected against the elements and time.

I played country, I played gospel,

I played classical, I played jazz,

A lazy drummer tapped percussion cymbals,

A guitarist strummed and plucked his strings,

Sultry saxophonists romanced the air,

While trumpets screamed and piccolos whistled.

I clapped my hands, lifted my heels,

And heaved my shoulders up and down,

While the 78's spinned like a carefree clock,

Returning me back to a place in time.

Down in the old mahogany victrola,

I found my grandfather once again,

Neatly trimmed hair, his brown fedora,

Shiny black shoes and Cuban cigars.

Sweet peppermint upon his breath,

And sounds that time had long abandoned.

Sitting on the floor with my grandfather's music,

I found a life I could hold onto,

Times and places, smells and memories,

Genuine love, and the art of music.

I flung back my head and snapped my fingers,

And swayed my hips to the rhythm of the bass,

And discovered my grandfather inside the victrola,

Loving my grandmother jazzy and good.

Among the Trees

You are there among the trees,

In the ridges of the wind,

In the early morning sap,

Running freely through my veins.

When the branches reach their fingers,

When they bend and stretch and bow,

When their arms are open to me,

I run to you among the trees.

You are there among the trees,

When the sunlight hits your bough,

In the cooling of the shade,

In the crackling of the leaves.

When the raindrops drench your foliage,

In the excess, in the spillage,

Amid the embryo and hatchlings,

I bathe with you among the trees.

Diamonds

(When reflecting on the Million Man March)
Thunder, lightning, black smoke, clouds.
All those diamonds, all those men!
Thunder, lightning, black smoke clouds,
All those men!

Thunder, lightning, black smoke, clouds,
All those diamonds, all those men!
Thunder, lightning, black smoke clouds,
All those men!

It rained diamonds, invaluable treasures,
So many diamonds they couldn't be measured.
All those men!
I ran, I laughed, I danced, I screamed!
All those diamonds, all those men!

Thunder, lightning, black smoke, clouds,
All those diamonds, all those men!
Thunder, lightning, black smoke clouds,
All those men!

Rich men, poor men,

Wise men, sure men,

All those men!

Young men, old men,

Good men, bold men,

All those men!

Thunder, lightning, black smoke, clouds,

All those diamonds, all those men!

Thunder, lightning, black smoke clouds,

All those men!

Triumphant men!

Courageous men!

Beautiful men!

Black men!

Thunder, lightning, ebony clouds!

Ebony diamonds! Ebony men!

Uncontaminated Merriment

Tiny feet scuttle along the flower bed. Laughter erupts out of her small belly like gushing volcanoes. Giggles trail behind butterflies and tiger lilies. The backyard is speckled with virgin discoveries and uncontaminated merriment.

Her innocent little eyes fill with imagination; her youthful spirit spills over in gleeful wonder.

The wrought iron fence is her castle, chrysanthemums make faces back at her, and weeds sprout legs. Her hands are small enough to cradle inside my own, but instead she grabs the wagging tail of the Bassett Hound. She is a toddler, a three year old, barely able to climb onto the jungle gym. Her preschool fingers summon my mature ones to propel her into the uninhibited air.

I lift her high, above my head, above my shoulders, above my fundamental rules. Her hands spawn wings. She is an airplane—born to fly. She spins and giggles and dreams and imagines and colors outside the lines.

Hatchlings

The brown cardinal squawks her bright red bill,

And dances on the fluted leaves.

Nearby her nest cradles new-born hatchlings,

Watching in simple splendor.

Accomplishments

I am completely accomplished. My resolve to have the biggest and finest and to run the distance further than the person beside me is diminished by the vigor I now find in birds and flowers and the joy of new mornings, breaking through thick clouds.

These are but small postings of the resolution I place within myself after years spent with measuring stick in hand, gauging my endeavors against those I would have to run a lifetime to keep pace with.

In this season of autumn when the sun sets early and darkness falls sooner, shortening the days and hours between now and then, I treasure the moments of sitting on the porch, refreshed in soul and spirit, looking out over the meadows beyond the "next big thing."

I leave the accomplishments and accolades and trophies and plaques on the wall to the young and the proud and the ambitious that do not tire of pushing themselves to the brink to reach the ultimate in status and titles and impressions as I once did before I tossed my measuring stick.

...Sensual

I remember those cold December nights and the hold you had on me then. You kissed me madly, singed my lips, and made the embers dance.

Wakening

I touch his lips on the pillow next to mine.

I watch him sleep peaceful sleep.

Hair grey as a wintry evening silhouetted against time.

Hands powerful enough to hold my dreams and pain.

I kiss him gently, he stirs.

Cottony soft and tender he awakens,

Mingles in my essence and unveils my secrets.

Two Saturdays One Summer

Two Saturdays, one summer I forgot,

I closed my eyes and forgot my pain.

Kisses were plentiful.

My breasts were young and tender again,

They tasted sweet between his teeth.

They were peaches filled with nectar,

Tender tomatoes ripe in their time,

Plush plums plucked from the vine,

Lush melons firm to his touch,

Honey dews lost in his clutch.

Summer ended and he left,

And my peaches returned to breasts again.

Strawberry Jam

I shut my eyes here in our bedroom,

The music is playing—something by Barry.

Pieces of toast slathered in strawberry jam still sit in the plate on the

nightstand, left over from breakfast this morning.

You nibble hungrily on the strawberry crumbs that fell between my breasts

before we decided to play hooky.

I love strawberry jam!

Thorns and Roses

I don't always know how to express my feelings.

Last night in the hot, summer heat when my anger was blazing,

It was my feelings for you that flamed the fire.

Isn't it strange that my most affectionate feelings grow thorns when all I

Want to do is kiss you softly, undress you gently,

And make love to you deeply with my hot, summer heat that is blazing.

Enough

I want to hold you so tight

That my fingers leave their prints

On your skin, on your bones,

On the memory of our love cries.

I want to hold you in the night,

In the dark—eyes peering through the blackness,

When you lean your head on my shoulders

And I move close, full and spent

In the moment that is enough.

Longing

Standing close enough to feel

Flesh and tendon,

I stepped back trying to obscure

The reality of touch against skin.

I shuddered when you pulled me close,

In the insatiable hunger of longing.

Red Dress

I bought a red dress,

Expensive and delicate and sheer.

Buttoned down the front,

See-through and lacey.

I put it on, wore it home, and waited.

He tore it off of me,

Like I was the only woman on earth.

I felt beautiful.

Lace and buttons flew.

Two, three, four buttons popped

And buried themselves in the carpet.

The red dress was ruined.

I was quenched.

Dogwoods

This winding path we took years ago,

The dogwoods bloomed,

Sweet with fragrant petals,

That touched each other the way

We once did in the perfumed scent of love.

The Morning After

The morning after sleeping limbs awaken,

Drooped branches straighten,

Revived by the moist dew.

Afterglow

I see the old pictures where I am smiling happier than ever before,

Love is in my eyes captured by a Kodak moment.

I can't recall the exact day I fell in love, but I remember rising early, singing and dancing and swaying my hips and going into the kitchen to cook up a mess of food.

Grits and sausage,

and Ham and biscuits,

and marmalade jams,

and pancakes,

and eggs and bacon.

I remember flour all over the granite counters, in my hair,

and down my cleavage,

and plundering in the cupboards for the fine china,

and candles and crystal,

and shining the silverware,

and the glass goblets,

and the showers we took with the sweetest smelling oils—the apothecary scents fuming the entire house,

and shaving my legs to make them smooth for when you'd place them in your lap again and curl my toes in the afterglow.

Encore

His eyes guard like crows scavenging over last night's meal.

I watch him behind me in the mirror sitting on the edge of the bed.

He slips his feet out of his shoes and waits for me to come close,

Then pretends to play the piano, caressing my keys again and again.

I pretend I have forgotten the song he played last night and force him to pound new notes in precision, bringing back to remembrance every interlude.

I applaud his repeat performance and upon the last note, I call for an encore.

Night Skies

Night skies dark and endless like black velvet,

Ruby wine dripping from my lips,

Seduced by his kiss on my mouth,

Love has come home tonight.

Waiting, longing, pleading,

I am a slave in this ebony space,

Helpless, breathless, needing,

Our passions rise.

Night skies blanket me and my love,

Peek not in the answering of our cravings.

Night skies send out your decree,

Command the morning to delay itself.

Pancakes and Syrup

I sit across from him at breakfast.

The syrup drips off the side of the pancakes,

In a slow, steady motion, sweet and thick and good,

Like the love we made last night—all night.

He reads his Wall Street Journal now.

I will not interrupt the morning ritual he reserves for facts and figures.

Instead I trace syrupy swirls in my plate,

My fingertips drip with the ooey gooey mixture of sweet molasses clicking against the porcelain.

He grabs my hands—licks and nibbles,

Then leaves his Wall Street Journal sopping up the syrup.

As Evening Comes

As the sun sets behind these gray, misty clouds and dawn turns to dusk,

So nears the end of this great love affair as this evening comes.

Dare we allow ourselves to give hope to feelings we know are long dead?

Or lie to ourselves and pretend not to notice the words that need to be said?

We laughed, we danced, imagined and dreamed and cried,

And made love and hated.

At what point do lovers turn into strangers?

What moment in time do friends become foes?

When did we throw in the towel and say love doesn't live here anymore?

Now as evening comes I wonder,

Answers elude me, I sit here and ponder,

How we laughed, and danced, imagined and dreamed and cried

And made love?

How has our laughter been turned into tears?

Our dance been shackled by heartache and fears?

When did we lose momentum to fly?

All that we do now is sit here and cry,

There was a time we both wanted more,

Each other was all we ever lived for,

When we laughed, and danced,

Imagined and dreamed and cried and made love and loved.

Needles in a Haystack

We fought our resistance against the harsh raindrops outside, as the storm settled in to trap us, holding us hostage in a nearby barn. Our eyes met briefly then looked away beneath the frantic sheets of rain drenching hair and hands and clothes.

We moved to a safe corner of the barn, the decayed roof protecting us from the elements as we held each other close in hopes that the hurricane would pass over quickly. Sweat permeated amid the damp smell of cedar wood and the grassy hay rolled neatly in the loft. Our eyes met once more and begged for the chance for two friends to abandon self-control. We did.

Clothes found a resting place across the bannister. Warm tongues met with the mixture of hot breath, foreign fluid, and kisses. Grazing atop the haystack, we devoured each other greedily, drawing from a deep well of urgent and demanding need. Outside the hurricane banged furniture against the lumber building. Inside thunder howled and lightning bellowed.

Changeling

I whisper into your spirit, you whisper into my heart.

You read me Gibran and Browning,

Making love to me on the pages with a poem and a song and a letter.

I take a cruise to get you out of my system,

Only to awaken to a confusing message you've left me on the phone.

When I am there with you, you push me away.

When I am away from you, you ask me to come.

You are a changeling, an endless metaphor.

You think because you will not say what you need to, no one else will.

You think because you are not reaching for me, no one else is.

Here in this remote place, where I am far away from your mixed signals now, someone else makes love to me on the pages and the bed.

Prohibition

Shall we have this dance?

Is it movement across the floor or something more?

Should not we leave before the music starts,

Before there is a knitting of our hearts?

Before we know the things we'll come to know,

Before we find that we are needing more?

Doesn't dancing bring us cheek to cheek?

Perhaps I should remain across the room,

Before you get a whiff of my perfume,

Perhaps we both should leave this dance alone,

Before I catch the scent of your cologne,

And after you return me to my place,

With nothing in between, not even space,

Will the dance between us really be enough?

Can we really say this dance will be enough?

Selective Amnesia

If I allow myself to remember you again,

Your sun drenched warmth dousing my skin,

Are we back there then?

Laughing, dancing, overpowering kisses,

Us making plans, us making wishes?

My caramel skin, you cinnamon brown man,

If I allow myself to remember you again,

Some memories though beautiful are better forgotten.

This Moment

He reaches for my hand, instructs me to be still,

Then pulls me close to him, so close, I feel his heartbeat.

Or is it mine?

Pounding.

Pulsating.

Palpitating.

Locked in his obstinate embrace,

He lingers his mouth just above my cheekbone,

Then puckers his perfect lips gently revealing the silhouette of a small letter o.

Our eyes meet.

I gasp!

I am pleasantly aware this moment is everything I imagined.

I wait. Anticipate.

He blows.

"Eyelash," he says.

Black Polished Wood

It's just a huge piece of black polished wood placed over in the corner of the parlor of our big, dusty house, with random sunlight beating down onto its black and white keys of black and white nothingness. There is no gray nor other colors in between until he plays and lets the music out, and fills this big, empty house with song, and makes the Priscilla curtains dance, and the walls vibrate to the bliss of sound.

When he strokes the keys with his touch his eyes light up in a way I can never get them to do for me. His mouth grins with the little smirk he brings when confident; hands caress the ivory with tender fingers making melody and song. I sit across the room on the velvet settee watching the two of them together for hours—I with my books, him with his piano, as he turns the keys into notes and notes into tunes, fondling crescendos and legatos in perfect harmony. He cracks the window just enough to let the music escape from his fingers, prowl the streets, and pounce on gullible prey who stop to listen. Then the keys return to ivory, and the melodies disappear, and the curtains stop dancing, and the notes scurry away. And he falls asleep in the lounge chair next to the black polished wood, in the dark, dim corner of this big, dusty house. Then I gather my books and crawl into bed and wish to God that I was his piano!

Extremities

She leaned over him, fluffing his pillow,

The old goose feather pillow,

Where his head lay in the cusp of the cotton folds.

Motionless, his eyes searched for something familiar, but found nothing,

Only the strangeness locked within them.

In one final gesture he reached out to her,

Hands fondled creamy white breasts,

Fingers remembered, then he died.

...Soothing

Today I am being nothing to everyone that I may be everything to myself.

The Old Soul

I wish you could see the way she makes something from nothing,

And creates a meal when you think there is no food in the cupboard.

And to hear her calm a little one in the middle of a tantrum,

Makes you want to crawl onto her lap and cuddle up against her soul.

Her spirit is as light as goose feathers,

Lips like crimson and cherry wine,

And when she parts them her words are as sweet as honey,

You can taste the syrup on every line.

Her hair is drenched in sweet vanilla,

The natural beauty peeps beneath the gray,

And those eyes, those discerning eyes,

Will make you spill your secrets out of your throat into her ears.

She is an old soul; she gives you the look.

In saying nothing she says everything.

Autumn

Although the memories fade away from her fingers,

She chronicles stories,

Delightful stories,

On the brittle pages of her mind.

Sightseeing

From across the street I watch them,

Sitting close, smiling, touching.

Old and gray, his arms around her,

Her eyes filled with longing.

My mind travels back to a time and place,

When being in love was enough.

The Preacher Preaches

He moves across the room with ease,

Words float in the air like glistening stars winding up into the brilliance.

Today it is simple—his life takes on a sudden shimmer; a silver purpose.

Staring through his reflection into tomorrow, the young boy's clothes he once donned fade into the dim vault of memory.

He is a man now—has been for a long time!

Noble, genuine, selfless, compassionate, loyal, and forthright,

The preacher preaches transforming everyone and himself into the familiar play of sunlight.

Turquoise blue anointing, green-yellow hues,

Spatter like brush on canvas and easel.

The air is flickering and electric, his words are exemplary.

His strides are hurried precision,

His feet are going somewhere.

Arms—branches wide with living leaves.

Eyes—shiny stars peering into the newness.

Loving, funny, and honest,

Benevolent, righteous, and gracious,

Baby boy in one arm, his bible in the other,

The mantle of both upon his shoulders,

The preacher preaches,

Transforming a child into a man and souls into God.

Whispers

Whispers of my ancestor's voices,

Crying, speaking, bleeding.

Undertones of the lineage I bare,

A flow of freedom's air blowing through my soul.

Liberated rain drops fall on my brow,

Unshackled words speak from my lips,

Whispers, the calluses from my ancestor's hands,

Release my spirit to soar.

The sigh of the motherland eavesdrops,

Listening to the blood drain off my feet.

Emancipated, my toes dance.

Unchained, my soul sings.

Unbound, my hands reach to create, to dream, to write.

Going

I discovered where I needed to go by going.

I didn't sit down and map out a plan.

I just took the next step that led to the next step that led to here.

In the going I arrived.

Swimming

You have waded long enough at the ocean's edge,

Testing the temperature, splashing your fingers.

Don't you think it is time to jump in and swim,

And rise up and down with the break of the waves

Carrying you out into the deep?

Dancing

My baby scoots to the top of the crib as I lift her from her cradle.

Her tears splash my night gown and I have no idea what to do to calm the little one. Perhaps it's the female bonding thing that prompts me to put on jazz. The three-month old already knows the pain of waking to nothing more than a wet diaper and colic.

I feel essential as oxygen and water and love here in the nursery with my baby crying and clutching my satin gown. If there was a way to make her young ears understand, I'd tell her how good it is to be a woman and cry for someone—how good it is to feel and be and have her own voice and stand in her skin. But all I choose to do is hold her close against my heart and hope that a dance with me in a dark nursery with yellow elephant wallpaper will be enough to get the message across and soothe her back asleep again.

Pulling from my bag of favorite tricks I dance around the room with my baby in my arms; her cries go quiet and soft as the spongy kisses I blow atop her silky black curls. Her breath small whimpers gurgling against my heart.

I tell her about mothers and daughters and sisters and love so strong and deep. I tell her about yearning and loving and serenity that grows within me.

I command her to be her authentic self, while I keep dancing,

Jazz in the background, my baby watching and I keep dancing.

I command her to love her authentic self while I keep dancing,
Jazz in the background, my baby cooing while I keep dancing.

I command her to live an authentic life while I keep dancing,
Jazz in the background, my baby sleeping while I keep dancing.

Jazz in the background, I keep dancing.
Silence in the background, music stops, and I keep dancing.

Grief Deferred

Today the sun shines brightly,

I allow it to bathe my skin.

Against this weeping willow I lean,

Sad thoughts beneath its drooping leaves.

Sun rays appear as quickly as the rain,

Evaporating moments I saved for sorrow,

I will rejoice in this picturesque day,

And mourn instead tomorrow.

Tranquility

Barren trees point to the sky,

Unfazed by winter's rage,

Calm in the knowledge that spring is on its way.

Feathers

The pain of being in love, at times, can seem unbearable.

Love lingers long after the hurt has healed,

Long after the scars have disappeared.

Oh that love was a chapter in a book that it might come to an end and be finished.

Love is not so—the effects of it lasts forever.

I saw myself crawl out of my cocoon and take wings.

Small wings, yet wings.

Feeble wings, yet wings.

And though I am apprehensive now, I know I will fly again.

With caution and with circumspect, but I will fly again.

And perhaps I shall look both ways before taking flight the next time,

But at least there will be a next time, and that is good!

Winter Storm

There is a season in every man's life,

When he passes through his winter storm.

When the sun decides to cease from shining

And dark, dreary days come to stay a while,

When cold, harsh winds beat against his domain,

Uprooting the things he has gingerly planted.

He must gather more seed, fertilize his ground,

Cultivate the soil, and prepare for harvest.

The winter storm shall surely pass.

It gracefully surrenders and falls asleep.

For to everything there is a season,

And after winter comes spring.

A Kiss Before Dying

Touch something gently, his lips, his mouth.

Touch something softly, his tongue, his cheek,

Touch something finally, his hands, his heart,

Then give to him a kiss before he dies.

Give a kiss before dying and let him go.

Give a kiss before dying and let him know,

In the kiss before dying that he was surely love.

Say good-bye in the kiss before dying,

Say good-bye in the way that you must,

Then set him free to fly among the clouds.

Touch something softly, his tongue, his cheeks,

Touch something finally, his hands, his heart,

And be sure to give a kiss before he dies.

Carry Me Home

Carry me on angel's wings.

Carry me on a joyful song.

Carry me on the prayers of saints.

Carry me home.

Carry me on the breath of hope.

Carry me on memories warm.

Carry me to the arms of Christ.

Carry me home.

Carry me in the eagle's nest.

Carry me from the place I love.

Carry me to my father's breast.

Carry me to home above.

Home

Familiar smells, a sincere touch, and longings that I have so much are home.

A kiss of love, a sister's smile and giggles from a tiny child are home.

A recipe and baking goods and ladies in the neighborhood are home.

Moments from so long ago, stories told and days of old are home.

A picture frame, the well-lit room, the smell of Nana's sweet perfume are home.

A rocking chair, the four post bed, and all the words that wisdom said are home.

An evening walk, a growing tree, and those who often think of me, are home.

Loved ones and my friends of course, laughter and a gentle voice are home.

Apple pie, the butter churn, and foods I find I often yearn, are home.

The old yard dog, the front porch swing, memories of so many things are home.

Yesteryears and days gone by, lingering thoughts and questions why are home.

The stucco house, the wooden stove, biscuits that I learned to love are home.

Mother's warmth on winter nights and words that make my spirit right,

On Sunday morn' the preacher's prayer and lots of hugs when I get there are home sweet home.

Playtime

"Play," said the squirrels.

For the lawn is full of children on the green.

Little feet are scurrying, hurrying upon the green.

Pink

My mother is staring at the easel—red, gray, white.

The colors are muted, mixed with peppermint hues.

Today she says she is inspired by the color pink,

But cannot remember where she laid her paint brush.

Her memory fades in and out now with traces of laughable lapses in between.

Patting my head, she asks me about the pink ribbons,

The ones that once held my ponytails.

I remind her I am 52.

She looks past me as if to collect the years,

Her thoughts dim candlelight losing its glow.

She inquires about my pink barrettes.

I remind her again I am 52.

Things are not as bleak as they seem,

Her smile is soft, sugary cotton candy, swirling into pink and white taffy.

My mother stares out the window now,

The clouds are pink-gray puffs shaping themselves into eyes.

She has located her paint brush,

And submerges the stiff bristles into the pastel colored cylinder.

One dip, then three pink strokes across the canvas.

Four dips, then six pink strokes across the canvas.

Tomorrow my mother will forget I am 52,

But today she remembers my pink barrettes.

This in itself is enough.

The Pardon

My grandmother's eyes meet mine,

They are sharp, jagged shears.

I watch her from across the room,

My building blocks growing taller, her gaze sterner.

My shoes are crossed at the ankle,

The patent leather glistening with the Vaseline I smeared atop of them,

Then trailed across the new shag carpet.

My grandmother moves toward me now,

Faster, quicker, foreboding.

I tremble and wait for her next action,

Words or belt, I know one or both are coming.

She grabs my small hands, snatches me up off the floor, front and center,

Looking me over like a crow scavenging for its last morsel.

Suddenly she pauses, her words and thoughts frozen in space.

I did that once myself she whispers, this will be our secret little one.

She smiles. I breathe.

The soft, cushiony kiss she plants atop my forehead reassures me she won't tell daddy.

She curls up on the window seat; I curl up on her lap, into the folds of a pardon.

Lightning Bug Evening

The sunlight scanned the oak tree leaves and just for a moment I thought,

I was seeing lightning bugs dance in the trees, the ones we caught as children.

Putting them into mason jars and watching them shine and glow,

We laughed and played in merriment but we tortured those bugs you know.

Puncturing holes in jelly jar lids to give those tiny creatures some air,

Pretending as if those holes somehow convinced us that we cared.

In spite of ourselves those lightning bugs shined like fireworks on the Fourth of July.

What fortitude, what attitude, what resolve for a glow in the dark fly.

Even as a tiny tot those bugs were teaching me a lesson,

Sparkle and gleam and glimmer and shimmer, how they left an impression!

At a distance I can hear mama yelling, telling us kids to come home,

As the sun set over the horizon, she was gently watching over her young.

Those lightning bugs were my guiding light that led me to mama's front door,

Where within those walls I ran in her arms and I played near her on the floor.

The wooden house has been left to me now, the china berry trees have died,

Many in the neighborhood have moved, for others we have mourned and cried.

But those lightning bugs they still come by and put on an afternoon show,

They sparkle and gleam and glimmer and shimmer and remind me of what I still know.

I find sweet comfort on this front porch swing as I sit here feeling real fine,

Thinking about mama and this little white house and the dinners that she made for nine.

May children discover the secret I learned when I grew up and was leaving,

That on a sunny day in the month of May at home there's a lightning bug evening.

Seasons

A friend is a beautiful, powerful person, who endures through all seasons.

Winter

On a cold, rainy day friends bring sunshine, and on a dreary, artic, winter evening, a friend is a warm afghan or a comfortable, old cardigan sweater you can wrap yourself in. Soothing like a cup of hot chocolate when your bones are chilled or a bowl of chicken soup during flu season, friends have a healing affect that goes through your veins and thaws your soul.

Spring

As refreshing as a breath of spring air, friends are like dogwoods and gardenia blossoms—they leave their potent aroma behind, always reminding you they are there.

Summer

Like a sprig of lemon in a cold glass of iced tea on a hot summer afternoon, friends add just the right flavor to your life, acting as a coolant during heated, sweltering moments.

Fall

Like fall leaves, friends come in all colors. Their hues run the gamut from yellow to bright orange, with hints of browns and reds in between. Whatever winds of change blow your direction; friends will always be standing by your side.

Friends have staying power!

Leap Frog

Something captured my attention,

When I turned to see,

Silent feelings of love,

Leaped inside of me.

...Sinister

Put the little girl to sleep so the woman can awaken. You can no longer keep company with her—do not travel in her circles nor allow her to travel in yours; she is immature and may embarrass you.

Backstage

Backstage I am waiting for my father to surface from the glistening, magical place beyond the sea of black leather instrument cases lying on the floor holding flutes and violins and cellos and clarinets.

Backstage I am waiting amongst the easy chatter of stagehands who look annoyed that I am there coiled in the red velvet chair next to the orchestra pit where Brahms and Chopin and Beethoven and I wait for my father.

The tired shuffle of father's footsteps draw closer as his boots hit against an open violin case placed randomly in the middle of the floor. The smell of wax oil on his hands mix with the tune of Fur Elise as he carefully lays down his black leather kit, then tucks away the soiled rag he uses to shine shoes.

Father grabs my hand tightly as we exit stage left, away from Brahms and Beethoven and Chopin and climb onto the city bus where spectators nod toward the back reminding us of our place. Father stares out the window into the cold, damp, night air. I lean my head against his shoulder and hum Chopin.

Investigation

I watch you analyze my poetry,

Searching for traces of my DNA on a poem you hope I wrote about you.

Nearby the dust covered quill leans against an unopened ink jar.

Ordinary Days

Blueberry pie without you here is ordinary.

Fresh snow, winter strolls,

Echo our laughter.

The mud room holds your boots,

Feet set on a different course.

My heart aches with all it holds.

Shelling Peas

We sat cross-legged outside on the front porch steps shelling peas—
laughing and talking like the old and young do when a good piece of gossip
is being imparted. Fireflies flickered around the lush vegetable garden – the
same garden that produced those peas.

Laughter died as the long, black car floated ghost-like down the red clay
road, kicking up dust clouds along the way. Mama swallowed the lump
in her throat, wiped her hands on her apron, then stood. Daddy's favorite
blue suit hung just inside the screen door waiting to be collected.

The black car came to a somber stop in front of the rickety brick steps.

The mortician exited, walked passed me, then followed mama into the
house. I grabbed a hand full of peas--click click plink ping. Minutes
later the mortician departed with daddy's lifeless suit dangling over his
shoulder.

Mama rejoined me on the front porch steps, picking up conversation where
she left off. Moisture filled the hot evening air—her shoulders shuddered,
head drooped. A small whimper erupted into a loud, volcanic shriek from
deep down betwixt the bone and marrow. Mama shelled a mess of peas
the day my daddy died!

Father Time

I mourned for him, yet for myself, upon the bench he sat,

The scene unfolding before my eyes was one I'd not forget.

For I had seen him years before, when I first came to town,

I was just a young man then, and he was fully grown.

And through the years I've seen him once or twice or maybe three,

He had become the measuring stick of what I would not be.

His hair was so much longer now, he sat upon the bench,

His clothes were soiled, his mane unkempt, his body smelled of stench.

Some had called him Homeless Man the one who liked to roam,

Eating out of garbage cans who never made a home.

But there I named him Father Time, a remnant of the past,

Reminding me of choices made, and how time goes by fast.

I looked beyond the Homeless Man, I peered into his face,

And wondered how that handsome man had gotten to that place.

I thought of all he could have been, the things he could have done,

And tried to figure out from him exactly what went wrong.

I mourned for him, yet for myself, I cried for Father Time.

For I was just a young boy then, and now I'm forty nine.

An Impatient Winter

Winter arrived in an impatient haste,

It was sudden and swift and would not wait.

And brought with it an untimely death,

Taking away my best friend.

Winter was gluttonous and covetous and rude.

It battered and shattered me and was crude,

Then kissed me and made up and sent spring!

Sleep Peacefully Tonight

Sleep peacefully tonight.

Let not unforgiveness be your bedfellow.

Pardon your adversary quickly whether he be a real or imaginary foe.

Dare not take unforgiveness to your bed,

Though you think him to be a passionate lover.

While at midnight his kiss is potent,

At daybreak he will leave you all alone with no reprieve.

Blinders

I loved him for what he wasn't,

Attentive, kind, gentle.

I was afraid to love him for what he was,

For fear of seeing the truth.

Mirror Image

Years, the gulf of time between daughter and mother.

Years, vantage points from one to the other.

Childish imaginations and a seasoned soul,

Fighting words between the young and the old,

Laughter spilling over in carbonated glee,

Two conjoined birds trying to free each other from themselves.

Years, the elongated mirror that patiently waits,

While mother and daughter and their debates,

Come face to face with their own reflection.

Then mother sees the daughter she once was,

And daughter sees a well-known face because,

Years ago when she wasn't looking she became her mother.

Prowling

Music roared from the piano,

Stalked its prey,

Found vulnerable spectators,

Pounced without warning.

Holding On

Sifting through mother's things,

Her entire life fits into a small suitcase,

Filled with love letters and costume jewelry.

For years, on hot summer evenings,

I watched her cry over a man who was unavailable.

He let go—she held on.

Orchid

On the clothesline his shirts hang outstretched.

I walk into their flimsy embrace; into their transparent folds of emptiness.

His footsteps are muffled on the carpet, trailing echoes of his exit.

Please won't someone explain the in-between of staying and going.

Won't someone tell me how to escape the ache of a definitive good-bye?

In the corner my tear-filled Kleenex expands into an orchid

That has fallen out of the empty vase.

 I Loved Once

I loved once.

With all of my heart and to the depths of me, I loved once.

I loved longing and needing and hoping and giving,

Watching and waiting and anticipating.

I loved once.

And then I lost gracefully.

I silenced my broken heart and commanded it not to speak of this again.

Resignation

The day dons a fresh new beginning,

Moments unseen, steps not taken.

Small strides, gigantic leaps, walks, runs, jumps.

The dayspring christens an unsung journey,

Taking stock of all that is,

Then the sun sets.

Gone are chances not taken,

Dreams aborted, hopes not awakened.

Afraid to kiss a virgin morning,

Afraid to let one's soul sing.

Resigning oneself to how things are,

And asking oneself what might have been.

Secrets

You hold them close like the stacks of books you press to your bosom,

Carrying them to your bed, placing them around the room. Some atop shelves; others on the nightstand underneath the soft glow of the bedside lamp.

Splashes of light cast silhouetted shadows on the walls above your head. The walls know your secrets.

Secrets you choose not to reveal, trickle across the terrain of love you thought you'd never give,

Across the landscape of a life you thought you'd never live,

Across the backdrop of tears you thought you'd never cry,

Across the vista of pain you thought you'd never sigh,

Across the pages of a poem you thought you'd never write,

Across the lips of words you'd never recite.

Words you keep tucked away believing they are your own.

Kind words, silent words, guilty words, tender words,

Blood stained words; the droplets know your secrets.

Laughing, mocking, shrieking, rolled tight like too many clothes stuffed in worn out luggage, waiting for the seams to tear enough for them to spill out onto the floor. The floor keeps your secrets—the ones you keep sweeping underneath the rug.

Naked Like the Trees

Naked like the trees in winter,

The leaves of my emotions have fallen.

I am disrobed, unclad, left bare, exposed,

Divulged, unwrapped, unveiled, disclosed.

No shelter, no shoulder, no shield.

Come spring.

Bring sprout and bud and bloom.

Bring blossoms and flowers and embryo,

And drape me and clothe me and hold me,

Until I find strength again.

Risk Takers

Every day the sun doth rise, beckoning, calling, summoning,

Extending an invitation to those who'd dare to come.

What good things shall the daybreak bring to those weary souls,

Who saunter out of bed each morn' to try and forget their woes.

Shall they play their cards today with the same safe, dull hand?

Or will they gather strength and throw their caution to the wind?

Or shall they again remain content with the card that life has dealt?

Or perhaps refuse and take a path in search of something else?

Or will tonight upon their beds where they began their day,

Say lay me down and go to sleep and tomorrow come what may?

And when the sun doth rise again and call to them and beckon,

Will they mope and grope and sigh because of spirits broken?

But here's to the risk takers, to those defiant souls.

Who awaken in their wonderment to defeat their inner woes.

Here's to the risk takers, to those courageous souls,

Who dare throw caution to the wind and to the wind they thumb their nose.

With

Every autumn I stand at the river bank,

Watching the snow geese fly away to unknown places,

Leaving me behind at the water's edge,

With wet sand oozing beneath my toes,

With liquid foam drenching my skirt tail,

With seashells crumbling between my fingers,

With waves splashing memories of you onto the salt-bleached landscape.

It comes to mind when I stand at the river bank,

With the ripples thrashing my heart against the rocks,

With the wind hugging my skin,

With the moist smell of the sea in my nostrils,

With the haunting voice of the Gulf Stream,

It comes to mind that the snow geese, like you,

Shall not come home with me again.

Broken

Limbs in the wind,

Shattered glass,

A million little pieces broken.

Battered, tattered,

Bits and pieces broken.

Bones in the wind,

Shattered glass,

A million little pieces broken,

Abused, misused,

All those pieces broken.

Thawed Frost

The candlelight in our hearts has diminished.

The thirst of our souls once quenched by the tender affection of touch,

Has become a dry, parched log smothered upon the hearth.

Like crackled winter leaves crumbling angrily between our fingers,

These fierce, howling winds have broken us.

Conversations drift away on the icy airstreams of resentment.

Remorseful words lay frostbitten beneath our lips.

This cold, cruel epoch is harsh; it has left us frigid and unbending.

Perhaps in spring when the frost has thawed,

The residue of our bitterness shall wash away in the first seasonal rain.

We both agree to put time on this.

To await the arrival of fresh new growth and embryo.

Who are you and I to toy with fate?

To assume she will bequeath to us another spring?

Hats and Gloves

Sunday go to meeting hats.

Controversies, little spats.

Lipstick, perfume, gloves and cats,

Pulling out their feline claws,

To scratch those who defy their laws,

Make-up, high heels, clutch bags, pearls,

They are dangerous little girls,

Anointing themselves as executors,

Judge and Jury and prosecutors,

Sunday go to meeting hats,

Disagreements and things like that.

Bibles, crosses, front row seats,

Vegetarians who don't eat meat,

Grudges, fights and little schisms,

All on behalf of the catechism.

Twilight

In the sunset of life, reflections.

Forgiveness comes easy now.

Man at his best state is vanity.

Absolving, he pardons his adversary,

Resolving, he pardons himself.

Contradiction

I tell myself I'm not in love,

So there are some things I don't speak of,

Because that's what I tell myself.

I tell my hands not to touch,

Because touching you is just too much,

So that's what I tell myself.

I command my eyes not to look,

Because if I look I may get hooked,

So that's what I tell myself.

I command my feet to walk away,

Because if they don't I just may stay,

So that's what I tell myself.

I tell myself I'm not in love,

So there are some things I won't speak of,

Because that's what I tell myself.

Foot Soldiers

In the closet his shirts hang buttoned down,

Drooping off expensive wooden hangers.

I lean my head against the shoulder of a starched, baby-blue silk arm,

And hold myself there in the emptiness.

On the floor his shoes line up like foot soldiers,

The worn leather, soft and comfortable,

I slip my toes inside the cushion membrane,

And bury my feet in the emptiness.

Tonight the sound of a slammed door,

With suitcases trailing behind echoes in my ear,

I lay on the floor beside his shoes,

And lean my head against their emptiness.

Child's Play

Spring arrives in all of its splendor,

Clapping its hands, dancing, and singing.

Dare not play until you work your dreams,

Until you toil the soil.

About the Poet

Shay Cook has been writing professionally for over twenty years. When she received her first check from New Writers Magazine in 1991, the acceptance letter from George Haborak, Editor and Publisher, affirmed her as a proficient writer, placing her among literary contemporaries. Since that time, Shay has harvested bylines in both small presses and national publications. Among her literary credits are non-fiction articles and poetry published in The Quill, Prominent Voices in Poetry, Writer's World, Office Professional Magazine, Chips Off the Writer's Block, Black Cat Poetry, Yesterday's Magazette, Shadow Poetry, and numerous Poetry Anthologies.

Shay Cook is the recipient of the Tampa Tribune Letter of the Day Editorial Award, The Hillsborough County Library Cooperative Lit Wit Poetry Award, and the Circle of Poets Award. As Featured Poet of WMNF Radio, The Westcoast Center for Human Development, the Plant City Urban League, and local, regional, and national venues. Shay has performed her work to hundreds receiving standing ovations, literary accolades, and invitations for reappearances.

Shay Cook is currently matriculating at the University of Phoenix where she is pursuing her Bachelors of Arts in Literature with a Minor in Management. She plans to continue to the Master's and Doctorate programs.

Shay pays her literary talents forward by teaching children and adults to read and write, as well as hosting creative writing workshops.

According to Shay, *"life is poetry in motion arousing the poet's pen!"*

Visit the Author and leave your comments at:

ShayCook.com

CPSIA information can be obtained at www.ICGtesting.com
Printed in the USA
LVOW11s0249200214

374411LV00002B/99/P

9 781475 940596